Revised and Expanded

Character Under Attack
& What YOU Can Do About It

By Carl Sommer

Complimentary Copy

Advance Publishing, Inc. • H o u s t o n

Advance Publishing, Inc.
6950 Fulton Street
Houston, TX 77022

www.AdvancePublishing.com

First edition: 2005
Second edition: 2006—revised and expanded

Library of Congress Cataloging-in-Publication Data

Sommer, Carl, 1930-
  Character under attack : & what you can do about it / by Carl
Sommer.-- Rev. and expanded.
      p. cm.
  Includes bibliographical references and index.
  ISBN-13: 978-1-57537-352-2 (hardcover : alk. paper)
  ISBN-10: 1-57537-352-1 (hardcover : alk. paper) 1. Moral educa-
tion--United States. I. Title.

  LC311.S62 2005
  370.11'4--dc22   2005008539

Table of Contents

Acknowledgment

I want to thank all those who have reviewed this book and offered their useful suggestions. My son John has been particularly helpful with his constant constructive advice. My sincerest thanks to him.

I would like to also express my appreciation for all the authors who have provided helpful information on why character is under attack and what one can do about it.

Chapter 1
Why I Am Writing This Book

Facing our nation today is a crisis of character. America leads the world in riches and power, but it is also at the top of the developed world in violent criminal activity, rates of imprisonment, sexually transmitted disease, abortion, and teenage suicide. In addition, children are lying, cheating, and stealing; and doing the same are business leaders and government officials. This has serious consequences for families, schools, and America's future.

Tony Snow, a Washington columnist with *The Detroit News* and former speechwriter for President George Bush, Sr., says about America's legacy that there is not a nation on earth that "takes greater pride in its moral heritage than the United States. George Washington expressed the Founders' loftiest hopes in his first inaugural address: 'The foundation of our national policy will be laid in the pure and immutable principles of private morality...the indissoluble union between virtue and happiness.'"[1]

Alexis Tocqueville, a French political writer and statesman, came to the United States in the early 1800s and studied our political system. From this experience he wrote his most famous work, *Democracy in America*. Tocqueville stated: "America is great because she is good, but if America ever ceases to be good America will cease to be great."

What has happened to character in America? Let's look at some facts. The U.S. Department of Justice says that in one year the federal government spends "more than $25 billion on direct expenditures for criminal and civil justice. State governments spend nearly $59 billion and local governments spend over $83 billion."[2] That's $167 billion that federal, state, and local governments spend for "police protection, corrections and judicial and legal activities."[3]

The Department of Health and Human Services Centers for Disease Control and Prevention states: "Sexually transmitted diseases (STDs) continue to be a major health threat in the United States. CDC estimates that 19 million STD infections occur annually, almost half of them among youth ages 15 to 24. In addition to potentially severe health consequences, STDs pose a tremendous economic burden, with direct medical costs as high as $15.5 billion in a single year."[4]

From the U.S. Government Office of National Drug Control Policy comes this report: "Illegal drugs cost our society approximately 110 billion dollars each year, according to the National Institute on Drug Abuse." The agency also states: "Accidents, crime, domestic violence, illness, lost opportunity, and reduced productivity are the direct consequences of substance abuse. Drug and alcohol use by children often leads to other forms of unhealthy, unproductive behavior including delinquency and premature, unsafe sex. Drug abuse and trafficking hurt families, businesses, and neighborhoods, impede education, and choke criminal justice, health, and social-service systems."[5]

If we boil just those figures down, the social breakdown costs taxpayers over $1,000 for every man, woman, and child in America in order to correct situations that are due primarily to a lack of character — money that could be better spent for education, highways, and better health care. In addition, due to lack of character we should not forget the pain and suffering to individuals and society caused by drug abuse, assault, robbery, rape, venereal diseases, illegitimate children, alcohol abuse, and other socially harmful activities.

Our schools are a prime indicator that our nation is suffering a character crisis. America in the industrial world is on top, but in educational achievement it ranks near the bottom. Why such a disparity? It will be demonstrated that the character crisis facing our nation has serious consequences for America's future success. We'll examine what went wrong and what can be done about it. But before delving into the problems and solutions, I want to share my experience of what prompted me to write this book, for it will reveal one of the major reasons for the rapid decline of character in today's society.

I left industry at the age of 40 to become a New

York City high school teacher. As I taught I became dismayed at the poor quality of education the students had received. While searching the permanent records of one of my tenth-grade classes concerning their reading and math scores, I discovered that over half of the class had a fifth-grade reading level or lower, and nearly half had only a fourth-grade math level.

In order to become a teacher, I had to go back to college to become certified. I attended Oswego State University, City College of New York, and New York University. NYU had the largest research library in New York City, and since I was on a leave of absence for the book I was writing on education, I spent countless hours at its library doing research. To discover what was happening inside New York City schools, I became a substitute teacher, teaching all grades from 1 to 12, in 27 different schools throughout the city. Some classes were orderly; however, I observed students climbing on desks, tables, and cabinets; throwing paper airplanes and balls in classrooms; running around the rooms and halls; harassing teachers; yelling; fighting; and knocking over chairs and desks. While substituting, I was threatened and cursed, had my foot stomped on, saw a teacher assaulted, and stopped numerous fights.

In my extensive research of schools, I discovered that schools across America had the same problems and worse, and many of the students were improperly taught. After devoting ten years researching for America's educational crisis and solutions, I wrote, *Schools in Crisis: Training for Success or Failure?*[6]

When I moved to Texas with my wife and five children, I went back to my former trade. In 1986 I began with my two sons Reliable EDM, a specialized machining company. Today it is the largest company of its kind west of the Mississippi River. Since I wrote about the educational crisis, now I wanted to provide materials to help solve the educational crisis. I chose to write picture books that would teach children the time-proven principles of how they can become successful.

As a businessman I knew the importance of first impressions. I took great pains that the books promoting virtues were of the highest quality, and that they were interesting and not preachy. As a parent of five children, a grandfather (currently fourteen grandchildren), as well as a teacher of children for many years, I reasoned that there would be a great desire for interesting storybooks teaching children the necessary virtues that lead to success. What I experienced shocked me. What I discovered has long-term consequences for children, parents, schools, and the future of our nation. It goes far beyond my writing experience; it's an issue that enters into the foundational principles of what makes a lasting and successful society.

My Passion

Since my machining business was successful, I left the work of running the company to my two sons. Now I could devote my time and energy to my passion—writing books. I was born in 1930, and since 1955 happily married. I served in the Marine Corps during the Korean War, was a high school teacher, assistant dean of boys, tool and die maker, foreman, tool designer, operations manager, and presently owner of three businesses. I taught a Junior Achievement economics course at Prague University in the Czech Republic, and served on the Texas State Board of Education Review Committee. I interviewed numerous students and parents as an assistant dean of boys, and hundreds of workers for employment as a foreman, operations manager, and business owner.

With my varied experiences I decided to produce interesting, high-quality character-building picture books that taught children the time-tested principles for success. To my great delight, parents, teachers, librarians, and especially children have enthusiastically endorsed the books. The entire "Another Sommer-Time Story™" series of 20 books and read-alongs have won these awards: Teachers' Choice Award™, Benjamin Franklin Award, ForeWord Magazine Book of the Year Award, and iParenting Media Award. To date we have sold over 200,000 copies, many to public schools and libraries.

In addition, *It's Not Fair!* won the Children's Choice Award, *The Ugly Caterpillar* won first place in the Benjamin Franklin Award for "Children's Picture Book," and *Today's Librarian* chose *Mayor For A Day* as the "Best Children's Picture Book." All books have been accepted by Accelerated Reader® and Scholastic Reading Counts®. Even though these books have been enthusiastically endorsed and won numerous awards, they received strong opposition from some of the leading review journals. I want to stress that what happened to me as a publisher is not the important issue; the important issue is why these character-building picture books were rejected.

That rejection was the crack in the door that spurred me to investigate why character is so strongly under attack in our nation. As I opened the door, I discovered there is something much larger than rejection of character-building books—there's a major philosophical battle raging in America concerning the erosion of values that has serious implications for our schools and society.

Character Under Attack!

Chapter 2
Strong Opposition

When I wrote the first six "Another Sommer-Time Story™" books and published the "Another Great Achiever" series, two full-color junior biographies from other authors, I submitted them in the proper fashion to the major reviewers. One of our main goals was to reach school librarians. The major reviewer for school libraries is the *School Library Journal*. Was I ever disappointed—*School Library Journal* gave the books they reviewed an extremely low rating.

That was a serious blow for us to enter the school market. I have no complaint over negative ratings; that's what review journals should do with books that don't meet proper literary standards. However, when I read this statement in *Children's Writer* in "A Reviewer's Eye View" concerning Trevelyn Jones, children's editor of *School Library Journal*, I was outraged. The article stated: "Jones says, however, that didacticism can hurt a book. 'Many very small new publishers think a children's book must have a moral. Those get creamed immediately.'"[1] My books were "creamed" or censored because they were didactic and taught moral lessons!

I wrote twelve more children's books, but I didn't send them to *School Library Journal* because main reviewers often get their reviews published on major booksellers' websites such as Barnes & Noble and

Amazon. However, I did send these books to other reviewers.

We sent some books to Publishers Manufacturing Association (PMA), an organization with over 3,500 independent publishers. Each year PMA sponsors the Benjamin Franklin Awards, and their "judges come from various relevant disciplines and are considered experts in their field." For first place in the "Children's Picture Book" category, they chose the book, *The Ugly Caterpillar*. We sent the same book to *The Horn Book Guide*. Along with this book, they reviewed *I Am a Lion*. This is their review:

> Another Sommer-Time Story series. A lion cub who bears a strong resemblance to a certain Disney character learns to accept his heritage. A caterpillar is teased for being ugly until she transforms into a butterfly. Both familiar stories are poorly written and gaudily illustrated. With dust jackets that list each story's specific moral qualities—such as self-esteem and respect for others—these cloying books are little more than didactic tracts in smiling animals' clothing.

The Horn Book Guide gave these two books, including the award-winning *The Ugly Caterpillar*, the lowest possible rating![2] (This book can be viewed free on our website.)

A sales representative from the *School Library*

Journal told us that the journal was writing an article about books that taught values. I thought that they may have had a change of mind, so we submitted my next two children's books: *It's Not Fair!* and *Noise! Noise! Noise!* Here's their review:

> The first book is a heavy-handed, flatly illustrated treatise on the need to have and follow a leader. When Buzzie declares it unfair that worker bees have to do all the work and convinces other bees to start a new hive with her, chaos reigns. Finally, she understands what Wizbee has been trying to tell her—that 'working with a leader brings happiness' and that 'it's important to let the leader tell the other bees what kind of work they should do.' The text is didactic to say the least and Budwine's illustrations are sophomoric and amateurish. No self-respecting child would be moved by this preachy lesson.[3]

However, *It's Not Fair!* won the prestigious Children's Choice Award sponsored by International Reading Association and The Children's Book Council where 10,000 children from different regions of the United States read and vote on their favorite recently published books. The *School Library Journal* review stated categorically: "No self-respecting child would be moved by this preachy lesson"; yet children choose this didactic book as one of their favorites!

Didacticism

Both *The Horn Book Guide* and *School Library Journal* criticized my books because they were didactic. *Webster's Collegiate Dictionary* defines didactic as: "a: designed or intended to teach; b: intended to convey instruction and information as well as pleasure and entertainment." You may be puzzled as to why books should be rejected because they intend "to convey instruction and information as well as pleasure and entertainment." You may ask, "Isn't this one of the purposes of education?"

Unfortunately, there's a strong bias against didactic books. *Writer's Digest* states that Simon & Schuster "Books for Young Readers" gives this advice to those wanting to submit books, "Please avoid problem novels, rhyming verse and didactic stories with morals."[4] Elaine Marie Alphin writing in *Children's Writer* about realistic fantasy says, "But this sort of realistic fantasy should never become a didactic exercise."[5] In fact, an admonition authors repeatedly hear when submitting material to publishers is that books shouldn't moralize.

I realize one can be heavy-handed and "hit them over the head" with a moral, but I'm speaking about books that convey instruction and information as well as pleasure and entertainment. To some this would be the ideal instrument for education—informative and interesting reading material that at the same time imparts constructive values. We received repeated comments from librarians that they can't keep our books on the shelves. One of the recurring comments we receive from children on why they enjoy our character-building books is that they teach a "lesson," they are didactic. Children want to learn. They want interesting books that teach them how to become successful.

It's rather amazing, if one wants to become a doctor, engineer, chemist, lawyer, or whatever occupation requiring a degree, one needs to take courses that are heavily didactic. Yet when providing children at the beginning stages of learning to read, one should not provide books that convey information and pleasure.

This is a major problem in education today, schools are not providing students with proper instruction and information. Many wonder how can students spend 10-to-12 years in school and still be unable to read and do basic math.

Today the educational crisis still persists. John Gehring in *Education Week* reports that the Organization for Economic Cooperation and Development stated, "Poor literacy skills among high school graduates and too few opportunities for adult education put the United States in danger of losing its competitive edge in a rapidly changing global market." Gehring adds: "The United States lags or has lost ground on several important education measures when compared with 29 other countries. In literacy, for example, the United States has the highest percentage of secondary school graduates who ranked below an international literacy standard." The article reports that only 10 percent of Finland's students lacked literacy skills; the United States, 59 percent![6]

The Information Age

Today, getting a proper education is becoming increasingly important. This is particularly evident when entering the business world. Dr. Joseph H. Boyett and his wife, Jimmie T. Boyett, coauthors of *The Guru Guide*, report: "We are in the midst of a great watershed change in which we are moving from an industrial to a knowledge economy....Knowledge work is replacing manual labor. By 2010, no more than 1 in 10 workers will be engaged in making or moving things."[7]

I can relate well to what's happening in industry. My company, Reliable EDM, is a high-tech machining company. Our CNC (computer numerical control) machines have the capability to cut parts for hours and even days at a time unattended. I've witnessed firsthand the dramatic changes in the machining industry. Today we have automatic tool changers, robots, and fuzzy logic where machines are able to think and make decisions. These technologies result in a less labor-intensive industry.

America needs an educated workforce. Today we live in a global economy, and competition is fierce. One may be against automation that eliminates jobs, but if America does not remain competitive, our economy will fall further and further behind.

Companies will go elsewhere to buy their products. *Inc. Magazine* states in "How China Will Change Your Business" this fact: "It is plainly understood that asking suppliers to lower prices is merely another way of telling them they ought to be prepared to meet the best price out of China."[8] This is the effect of global competition.

David Gergen, editor at large for *U.S. News & World Report* speaks about the alarming way "we are educating our young men and women. Back in 1983, a national education commission famously concluded that our schools faced a 'rising tide of mediocrity.' Educators, governors, and CEOs quickly swung into action, and we have been trying to improve K-12 classes ever since."[9] Gergen then reports what happened 22 years later:

> When the nation's governors gathered recently for a national "education summit," their partnering organization, Achieve, presented data showing that the high school dropout rate has actually gotten worse since 1983! Of the kids who now reach ninth grade, 32 percent disappear before high school graduation. Another third finish high school but aren't ready for college or work. This, about two thirds of our students are being left behind, many of them low-income and minority kids. Only the upper third leave high school ready for college, work, and citizenship.[10]

Then Gergen states what needs to be done to strengthen our nation:

> We should be not only alarmed but ashamed. Our leading figures—the presidents, for example, of the Massachusetts Institute of Technology, Harvard, and Yale, along with the CEOs of Microsoft, Intel, and IBM—must rally Washington and the country to a revolutionary overhaul of public education. In our founding years, Americans were among the most literate people on Earth, and that put us on an upward path. The education of our young has always been a key to our greatness. Will we now rescue the next generation or condemn it to second place?[11]

We live in an information age where obtaining knowledge is vital for America's future economic success. One of the critical issues is to provide students the kind of books they need to learn the character principles of how to obtain knowledge, such as discipline, diligence, perseverance, proper work ethic, respect, self-discipline, and responsibility. Yet there are those opposing character-building didactic books—the very kind of books our students need.

But why should teaching children such character principles be attacked? These books are attacked because some educators believe children should not be influenced by outside forces; instead, children should be determinators of their own value system.

Children as Determinators

There is a trend in America that teachers should avoid influencing children under the premise that children themselves should be their own authority. Some advocate that children should even go against parental authority. John Leo in *U.S. News & World Report* states:

> Told by schools to construct their own value system, students are often led to challenge parental values or to dismiss almost any adult objections as illegitimate. Last week, a friend here in New York saw this in action. When she asked what her young child's school was going to do about a wave of bullying, including pushing classmates down a flight of stairs, the head of the school said no action would be taken because "children at this stage in their development do not welcome adult intervention."
>
> Dan Mack's strong new book, *The Assault on Parenthood: How Our Culture Undermines the Family*, makes the case that the crisis of the public school system is not simply the familiar one of academic failure. It's also that a new ethic, dismissive of parents and traditional values, has descended on the schools.[12]

John Leo then reports: "In the media, parental objections to all this usually come under the heading of condoms, school prayer, and the religious right. But behind the media screen, parents of all political stripes are getting the message, and pressure is building." Leo continues by directing our attention to "one of our best public intellectuals," Alan Wolfe, and his dire warning, "If social trends can be proclaimed based on my personal experience, suburban public schools are about to face the same precipitous declines in enrollment suffered by urban ones."[13]

Across the nation parents are greatly upset about what's happening in schools that encourage children to challenge their authority and to be their own determinators of their value system. Many more parents would be alarmed if they only knew what their children were being taught. When parents object to what's happening, they are accused of being bigoted and intolerant. Because of issues like these, many parents want charter schools created or to be provided with vouchers so they can choose their own schools. Others in their frustration are opting out of the school system altogether and with great sacrifice send their children to private schools; others are home schooling their children so they can teach the values they deem important. America is in the midst of a philosophical battle that has serious repercussions for our children and our nation.

Chapter 3
The Philosophical Battle

The philosophical roots plaguing our educational system today are the same when in 1984 I wrote, *Schools in Crisis: Training for Success or Failure?* In summarizing the problems facing schools, I wrote that what the American public had to understand is the root cause of the school crisis. The crisis was a result of a conflict between two ideologies. One advocates permissiveness, freedom without responsibility, instant gratification, no tests, no homework, free and open classrooms, automatic promotion, profane textbooks, parental disrespect, laxity toward misbehavior, lowering of standards, situational ethics, maximum individual autonomy, sexual license, euthanasia, right to suicide, and anti-Americanism.

The other belief system favors discipline, *in loco parentis*, law and order, freedom with responsibility, work ethic, academic excellence, knowledge of the basics, tests, homework, achievement promotion, parental respect, decent textbooks, sexual purity, and patriotism.

The conflict was between naturalism and the traditional American value system. I came to realize that those opposing character-building materials have the same philosophical roots as naturalism. Naturalism believes that everything can be explained by natural law without any moral or spiritual significance. Values therefore are relative and situational. There are no moral absolutes. Since there are no moral absolutes and values are situational, acts that give the individual pleasure are the decisive test of whether the act is good or evil.

One of the outgrowths of this naturalistic philosophy is humanism. The humanists produced two manifestos describing their beliefs. The first was published in 1933, and because of new events a second manifesto was published in 1973. A careful reading of these documents reveals their destructive philosophy. Following are some excerpts from *Humanist Manifesto* published in 1973:

Ethics: We affirm that moral values derive their source from human experience. Ethics is *autonomous* and *situational*, needing no theological or ideological sanction.

The Individual: *The preciousness and dignity of the individual person* is a central humanist value. Individuals should be encouraged to realize their own creative talents and desires. We reject all religious, ideological, or moral codes that denigrate the individual, suppress freedom, dull intellect, dehumanize personality. We believe in maximum individual autonomy consonant with social responsibility.

In the area of sexuality, we believe that intolerant attitudes, often cultivated by orthodox religions and puritanical cultures, unduly repress sexual conduct. The right to birth control, abortion, and divorce should be recognized. While we do not approve of exploitative, denigrating forms of sexual expression, neither do we wish to prohibit, by law or social sanction, sexual behavior between consenting adults. The many varieties of sexual exploration should not in themselves be considered "evil."[1]

Once this naturalistic humanistic philosophy of moral relativism is understood, that truth and values are autonomous and situational and never absolute, it becomes clear that its teaching has permeated not only our schools but also our society. This philosophy continues to be the archenemy of our traditional value system that there are moral absolutes.

Fruits of Moral Relativism

Today many of our youth have embraced the relativistic philosophy, "If it feels good, do it." Self-expression and self-fulfillment are their aims in life. When some children fall prey to this way of thinking, it can lead to actions that are rationalized by the thought, "Might makes right," and "If I receive pleasure at your expense, so be it. So what if I stab you in the back for your new sneakers? I could care less about your pain. I'm happy, and that's what counts."

Our society has raised a self-indulgent, hedonistic group of youths. We shouldn't wonder why sex violence is so rampant and our prisons are full. Youth are doing what they were taught—they're making themselves happy. They're not interested in anyone except themselves. "If it feels good—it's good." No value is superior to another value.

Relativists want to do whatever brings them ultimate happiness without guilt—that's utopia. Unfortunately, the belief of self-fulfillment at any cost has produced Hitler, Mao Zedong, Stalin, Pol Pot, and other ruthless dictators who killed millions to fulfill their utopian dreams. But remember, these ruthless dictators killed millions in their belief that what they did would benefit their concept of society. Shouldn't we be tolerant of them because they did what they believed would help them? This question is ridiculous, but there are those who defend this philosophy.

What is the result of a hedonistic philosophy where personal satisfaction is the end objective in life? It undermines the structure of a society. Look at some of our youth who have chosen drugs, alcohol, promiscuous sex, and a life of crime instead of work for sustenance. Sadly, what brings us to our senses is when we experience firsthand the shocking results of this indulgent lifestyle when violent gangs roam our streets and students without remorse kill students and teachers. How many of these incidents will it take to wake up Americans to see the ruinous effect of their departure from the values that made our nation great?

Don't for a minute think these violent kids don't have a moral system. They may not be able to express it philosophically, but they're looking out for number one—they want to be happy at any cost—and that's what counts. This is not a new concept. There's a well-known philosopher, Friedrich Nietzsche, professor at the University of Basel, who advocated this view. William Kilpatrick, Professor of Education at Boston College, in *Why Johnny Can't Tell Right From Wrong,* tells about the morality Nietzsche advocated:

> As far as Nietzsche was concerned, morality was good only *for* ordinary people. It was an invention of Jews and Christians. He called it "slave morality." His own interest was focused on an extraordinary type of individual: what he called the superman, or, in German, *Übermensch.* The superman does not allow himself to be fettered by conventional morality. He is even beyond the categories of good and evil. He is a law unto himself. He

doesn't subscribe to a received set of values, but rather, he creates his own values out of the power of his will.

With Nietzsche, morality goes into the dustbin of history. What replaces it is not pure reason but pure will. Life in Nietzsche's view is a meaningless, chaotic void: there is no God, no purpose or plan; nature and the universe are indifferent to man. The only meaning or order life has is that which is imposed on it by strong individuals. "What is good?" asks Nietzsche. "—All that heightens the feeling of power, the will to power, power itself in man. What is bad?—All that proceeds from weakness."...

Prior to Nietzsche, philosophers had always tried to justify moral decisions in reference to something else—either God or natural law or reason or nature. With Nietzsche, decisions become self-legitimating.[2]

This hedonistic, self-created value system proclaiming that all values are arbitrary has brought havoc to our world. Humans with this philosophy have no intrinsic worth. Kilpatrick tells what happens when Nietzsche's disciples act out this philosophy:

When Adolf Hitler first met Benito Mussolini, he presented him with a gift of the collected works of Nietzsche. It was an appropriate memento. Hitler's ideas about life and politics were largely derived from Nietzsche. Hitler subscribed to the Nietzschean idea that superior people have an inborn right to rule. He also believed they should be free of any bondage to worn-out moralities. Along with Nietzsche, he despised "slave morality"—the Judaeo-Christian ethic. Although Nietzsche was not anti-Semitic in the way Hitler was, he clearly paves the way for anti-Semitism by pointing to the Jews as the source of the inhibiting moral system that had crippled the vital impulses of European peoples. Hitler was merely echoing Nietzsche when, in a speech, he asserted, "Conscience is a Jewish invention. Like circumcision, it mutilates a man."[3]

The world witnessed the destructive force of Hitler and Mussolini during World War II. Hitler put millions of Jews and other undesirables into gas chambers in order to create "his" world. Fortunately, America rose to the challenge, and with the help of its allies defeated Hitler.

America at that time had a well-entrenched value system. Schools taught values and streets were safe. Then the relativistic forces began to attack our traditional value system of promoting character in children.

A void was created, and in its place the philosophy that morality is situational and moral absolutes are no longer valid became the new value system. The result? Children were encouraged to choose their *own* values. Many chose antisocial values, and when they matured they filled our prisons. *Houston Chronicle* provides this shocking report: "Over the past two decades, the number of adults in the corrections system has tripled, so they now make up 3.1 percent of the country's adult population, compared with 1 percent in 1980, said Allen J. Beck, a chief researcher with the Justice Department's Bureau of Justice Statistics."[4]

Mushrooming of Criminals

Something is happening in America that is producing this mushrooming of criminals. It was not always so in our nation. Can we not see a correlation between attacking character and the filling of our prisons with criminals? Teddy Roosevelt said, "To educate a person in the mind but not in morals is to educate a menace to society." We certainly have a menace in our society today. Wouldn't it be much wiser to teach children the morals required to become a productive and contributing citizen? But this would present a great problem—we would have to utilize didactic materials!

So what's the solution to keep criminals off the streets? Many say, "Lock them up." We're happy — crime is going down while prisons are filling up. How many billions of dollars of taxpayers' money would be saved if we had chosen to train children with proper values who are now adults in our prisons? Also, instead of criminals, we would have law-abiding citizens paying taxes! Fortunately, today there are many who are demanding character education be taught in our schools. Unfortunately, entrenched forces are opposing such moves. What should be done?

Wayne Scott, head of the Texas penal system, the nation's second largest, said Texas needs to pay attention to four- and five-year-old children. "If you want to address the (crime) problem in the long term," reported Scott, "it gets around to...looking at at-risk children and identifying those individuals very early on and trying to influence them in a positive direction." Then he added, "I think you have to look at pre-kindergarten, kindergarten, first grade. You really have to put a lot of emphasis on children. Those are the formative years."

Scott stated that his 25 years in the Texas Department of Criminal Justice shows those who end up in prison had "established criminal records by the time they were 10 or 11 years old." Concerning substance abuse, Scott pointed out that most at-risk children had "problems very early in their lives—by 8, 9 or 10."[5]

What a common-sense solution: Train children early to develop positive values. What better way to do this than by insisting that every school has an atmosphere of character and provides students with materials and programs promoting virtues?

Another issue facing our youth today is the lack of heroes. Today, many of our past heroes are belittled and every vice that can be brought up against them is magnified. Instead of revealing the noble qualities these individuals achieved, they are cut down. In their place are people who have achieved monetary success. Whether sports stars, music celebrities, rap singers, porno stars, or whoever, if they make money—that's success. Why not individuals as George Washington, Abraham Lincoln, Benjamin Franklin, George Washington Carver, Helen Keller, or Mother Theresa? Men and women of character—that's the kind of people we should hold up as heroes.

Regrettably, many in leadership positions have embraced the relativistic philosophy. As a result, America has lost its heroes and moral direction. *U.S. News & World Report* in the article "The American Uncivil Wars—How crude, rude and obnoxious behavior has replaced good manners and why that hurts our politics and culture," states:

From one end of the country to the other,

parents and teachers complain of the lack of civility among children and the disrespect they show their elders. The problem cuts across all class and racial lines. In the recent survey of educators by the American Association of School Administrators, the teaching of the golden rule—treat others as you want to be treated—was found to be an urgent necessity.[6]

David G. Myers, in the article, "Wanting More In an Age of Plenty," presents these startling facts:

During most of the post-1960 years, America was sliding into a deepening social and moral recession that dwarfed the comparatively milder and briefer economic recessions. Had you fallen asleep in 1960 and awakened today (even after the recent uptick in several indicators of societal health) would you feel pleased at the cultural shift? You would be awakening to a:

Doubled divorce rate.

Tripled teen suicide rate.

Quadrupled rate of reported violent crime.

Quintupled prison population.

Sextupled (no pun intended) percent of babies born to unmarried parents.

Sevenfold increase in cohabitation (a

predictor of future divorce).

Soaring rate of depression—to ten times the pre-World War II level by one estimate.[7]

Something has drastically changed in our nation. Mortimer B. Zuckerman, editor-in-chief, *U.S. News & World Report*, in an editorial on "Where Have Our Values Gone?" had this to say:

Social dysfunction haunts the land: crime and drug abuse, the breakup of the family, the slump in academic performance, the disfigurement of public places by druggies, thugs and exhibitionists. Are we now, to use Sen. Daniel Patrick Moynihan's phrase, 'defining deviancy down,' accepting as part of life what we once found repugnant?

We certainly seem to have lost the balance between societal rights and individual freedoms...Gone are the habits America once admired: industriousness, thrift, self-discipline, commitment.

The combined effect of these sicknesses, rooted in phony doctrines of liberalism, has been to tax the nation's optimism and sap its confidence in the future. And it is the young who are strikingly vulnerable. They are being deprived—like no previous generation—of the emotional comfort and moral nurturing provided by the traditional family. Instant gratification is the new order of the day. Personal impulses, especially sexual, are constantly stimulated by popular music and television, with other mass media not far behind. TV and music often seem to honor everything that the true American ethic abhors—violence, infidelity, drugs, drinking—and to despise everything that it embraces—religion, marriage, respect for authority. No wonder it is difficult to sustain parental values and parental continuity....

The nation's hunger for a public commitment to social and moral betterment is not a simple nostalgia for the greater simplicities of yesteryear; the clock cannot be put back. It is a profound and anxious desire to arrest decay.[8]

What a shocking statement on what's happening in America. In addition to the moral breakdown is the question of what businesses will do to earn money. Sex sells, and there are businesses that will stoop to any level in order to sell their products. In spite of this, there's a great desire for social and moral betterment; however, there are active forces resisting.

Censorship

If you believe in the philosophy of relativism in which there are no moral absolutes and each situation determines what value should be chosen, then you would censor books promoting traditional values because of the powerful influence reading materials have on children. William Kilpatrick, Professor of Education at Boston College, in *Why Johnny Can't Tell Right From Wrong*, states:

In recent years a number of prominent psychologists and educators have turned their attention to stories. In *The Uses of Enchantment* (1975), child psychiatrist Bruno Bettelheim argued that fairy tales are a vital source of psychological and moral strength; their formative power, he said, had been seriously underestimated. Robert Coles of Harvard University sity followed in the 1980s with three books (*The Moral Life of Children, The Spiritual Life of Children,* and *The Call of Stories*) which detailed the indispensable role of stories in the life of both children and adults.[9]

How does this relativistic philosophy play out in the real world? We sent a number of our first picture books to various librarians across America to get their reactions. We had a number of responses. Two in particular vividly portray the issues between two opposing ideologies. Let me first introduce the reviewed book, *No One Will Ever Know,* which shows the consequences of disobeying parents:

> Teased by their friends that no one will ever know what they were about to do, Johnnie and Janie squirrel ignore their parents' warnings about the big, bad wolf. Wanting big, delicious acorns, they lie to their parents and sneak out one night with their friends to Mr. Smith's farm. However, the delightful meal suddenly ends with them being chased by a very hungry wolf. The wolf attacks Johnnie and bites off his tail. Johnnie finally learns: To disobey is wrong, even when you think no one will ever know.

I have two signed statements allowing me to use the following comments. They reflect the philosophical battle being waged. The first one is from Deborah Gitlitz, a youth service librarian from the state of Washington:

> Carl Sommer's picture book series *Another Sommer-Time Story: Fun Time with Timeless Virtues* is a disappointingly transparent effort to disguise rigid moral lessons as "fun" stories.

Sommer's tone is patronizing and righteous; his writing is repetitive and perfunctory; his characters are cardboard and insultingly gender-stereotyped; and his plots are cannibalized from far more successful folktales and fables. The accompanying illustrations are heavily cute. Implicit in the text and illustrations (along with the overt lessons, such as "Obey your parents without question") are messages such as: that males rule the household; that lessons should be painful; and that everyone is middle class and probably white, even the squirrels. Children are unlikely to tolerate such obviously preachy lesson-tales.[10]

The next comment is in stark contrast. It is from Jenny Holloman, a media specialist from Georgia:

Excellent for character education, *No One Will Ever Know* teaches the importance of being obedient and following rules. Young Johnny and Janie squirrel are tempted by their older friends to go for the "big acorns" at Mr. Smith's farm. They set out on an adventure that not only causes harm from the Big Bad Wolf, but teaches them that they should always listen to Mom and Dad. "To disobey is wrong, even when you think no one will ever know."

The beautiful illustrations make this one a winner![11]

One wonders how Gitlitz could ever get from a storybook about squirrels that they were middle class and probably white. But notice especially one objection from Gitlitz is the overt lesson, "Obey your parents without question." To Gitlitz, children, as autonomous individuals, should question parental directives. This translates to, "What right do parents have to insist that their children obey them?" Parents, according to this teaching, should let children choose their own values.

Smoke Screen

You have previously been presented with the comments against didacticism from review journals. But rejecting books because they are didactic is just a smoke screen for rejecting books teaching positive virtues. When books support values the reviewers believe in, such as homosexuality, then books can be didactic. Following are some reviewers' comments about two children's books promoting homosexuality.

The book, *My Two Uncles,* by Judith Vigna, talks about the girl Elly who has two uncles. Her true uncle is Uncle Ned who has a gay friend called Uncle Phil.

Elly is puzzled why Grampy doesn't want his son Uncle Ned to come to his fiftieth anniversary party because of his gay friend.

School Library Journal says Elly's "father then explains why Grandpa is angry, telling Elly that he respects Ned and disagrees with Grandpa. Uncle Ned refuses to come to the party alone, and gives the gift to Elly to present. When Grandpa opens it, he expresses regret for having rejected his son. The rather ordinary, cartoon-style watercolor illustrations are a simple accompaniment to the story. There is a broad definition of homosexuality as love between two adults of the same sex, like that found in a traditional marriage...Parents seeking to explain a homosexual couple's relationship may find this book useful."[12]

Publishers Weekly comments about another book promoting homosexuality, *Daddy's Roommate* by Michael Willhoite: "This picture book is an auspicious beginning to the Alyson Wonderland imprint, 'which focuses on books for and about the children of lesbian and gay parents.' That the venture is being undertaken is in itself commendable: consciousness-raising concerning gay issues can handily begin at an early age with the help of books such as Willhoite's.... 'Mommy says Frank and Daddy are gay'—this new concept is explained to the child as 'just one more kind of love.' Willhoite's cartoony pictures work well here; the colorful characters with their contemporary wardrobes and familiar surroundings lend the tale a stabilizing air of warmth and familiarity." [13]

School Library Journal points out about the same didactic book promoting homosexuality, "It will be useful for children in similar situations for helping those from heterosexual families understand differences." [14]

In accordance with the philosophy of relativism, producing didactic books advocating homosexual behavior is considered acceptable and even commendable. The hypocritical stance of some reviewers is quite apparent. The issue is not whether books are didactic; the issue is whether the books meet the philosophical standards of the review journal. The sad part is when reviewers label a book promoting values as "didactic," immediately the red flag of rejection is raised; there's no need to further evaluate the book for art, content, or interest. The end result is a scarcity of character-building children's books.

But do we comprehend what goes on during many homosexual acts where sex takes place between multiple partners? Kermit Rainman, social research analyst for Focus on the Family, reports in "Silence v. the Truth," how dangerous homosexual acts can become for those practicing this behavior:

Data from the Centers for Disease Control and Prevention reveal that the vast majority of cases of HIV transmission are through homosexual contact. Young men are especially at risk. Indeed, at least half of the 40,000-50,000 new HIV infections annually are among people under 25. Tragically, one out of three 17-year-olds who identify themselves as homosexual will be HIV positive or dead from AIDS by age 30.[15]

Should schools be advocating this behavior under the guise of tolerance as an alternate lifestyle for children? Won't students be encouraged to experiment with this socially accepted behavior by non-judgmental teachers? How can anyone advocate such a destructive behavior when "one out of three 17-year-olds who identify themselves as homosexual will be HIV positive or dead from AIDS by age 30"? We need to be compassionate and realize the suffering that many of these individuals will encounter because they practice this lifestyle.

Chapter 4
Anticulturalism

A modern trend today is anticulturalism: the belief that children as autonomous individuals should be left alone and even challenge the current culture. John Leo in *U.S. News & World Report* comments:

> Hymowitz argues that as child-liberation ideas entered the mainstream, they hardened into a philosophy she calls "anticulturalism"—the idea that socializing children and attempting to mold the character of the young is a wrongful use of power by the strong against the weak. Children should develop independently of the prevailing culture and even in opposition to it. This idea is radical, because it forbids what all cultures have assumed they must do: transmit cultural values from one generation to the next....
>
> Hymowitz demonstrates how widely this improbable philosophy has managed to spread. "Anticulturalism," she writes, "is the dominant ideology among child development experts, and it has filtered into the courts, into the schools, into the parenting magazines, into Hollywood, and into our kitchens and

family rooms." It boils down to the notion that children should be allowed to develop on their own; that parents and schools should stimulate and encourage but otherwise stay out of the way. The emergence of the moral self must not be quashed by what Harvard psychologist Carol Gilligan calls the "foreign voice-overs of adults." Children are not to be raised, but simply allowed to grow.[1]

Today this influence has created a strong movement in educational circles that it's wrong to attempt to mold the character of children. Now it becomes clear why these individuals oppose character-building materials while praising materials that promote autonomy.

What is your philosophical viewpoint? Do you believe children should be totally independent to develop their own set of values, or do you believe children should be taught values from parents and society about how to make proper choices? If you believe children should be autonomous, you'll despise character-building materials. If you believe children should be trained concerning values, you'll praise such materials. This is what my extensive research and personal experience have revealed—people either hate or love materials promoting values.

Publisher's Dilemma—Please or Perish

I realize going public and exposing review journals concerning their position about materials teaching morals is an unwise strategy for a publishing company. To enter the school market, I should please journals such as *School Library Journal, Publishers Weekly,* and *The Horn Book Guide.* In addition, not only are the negative reviews printed in the review journal, but they are also published on various booksellers' web sites. So one can realize the tremendous influence these reviewers wield.

What is the result of this bias against character education children's books? From our research of asking librarians nationwide, "Is there a scarcity of character education children's books?" the overwhelmingly response is, "Yes."

Listen to Dr. William J. Bennett describe his experience of the shortage of character-building materials when he was director of the Office of National Drug Policy under President George H.W. Bush:

I visited about 140 communities and heard over and over a much different concern. Whether I was talking to teachers, school administrators, parents, cops or judges, they wanted to know: Who's raising the children? What kind of character do our kids have? Who's paying attention to their morals? A judge in Detroit once said to me, "When I ask young men today, 'Didn't anyone ever teach you the difference between right and wrong?' they answer, 'No sir.' And you know, Mr. Bennett, I believe them. It is a moral vacuum out there." I remember teachers in the public schools asking, "Can you help us develop some materials that we can use with our kids to teach them right from wrong?" Isn't it ironic? The public schools of this country, which were established principally to provide common moral instruction for a nation of immigrants, were now wondering if this was possible.[2]

Why is there such a scarcity of character-building books when so many want them? One must realize publishing companies must print books bringing them profit; otherwise, they'll be forced out of business. The larger publishers know the position of major review journals, so they either please the reviewers or perish.

What should I do? My desire is to publish materials teaching children principles on how they can become successful. Should I yield or buck the system? I made the decision not to submit. To date, many of our books have been translated into foreign languages, and we've sold over 200,000 of these books, many to public schools and libraries. We have also sent a free copy of the first edition of *Character Under Attack & What You Can Do About It* to every public elementary school in America, over 55,000 schools.

Child-Centered Education

Children should be provided with a child-centered environment that respects their inherent nature and produces optimal development and growth. The focus of this education should be to provide materials and instruction that is best for the child. The question emerges, "What is the best educational environment for maximizing optimal development and growth for children"?

Some believe that if you let children grow up naturally they'll turn into beautiful flowers. It's like planting a garden with flower seeds. There are two options: Leave the garden alone and hope for the best or watch over the garden by weeding, fertilizing, and watering. Everyone knows what would happen if one doesn't take care of the garden. One will have a garden of weeds. That's exactly what's happening today in many so-called "child-centered" permissive environments. Many of these educators pride themselves on how they love children, but in reality they are destroying them by not providing children with an education that will benefit them for their future.

Christiana Hoff Sommers, a former philosophy professor and one who specializes in ethics and contemporary moral theory, stated, "Common sense, convention, tradition, and even modern social science research all converge in support of the Aristotelian tradition of directive character education. Children need standards, they need clear guidelines, they need adults in their lives who are understanding but firmly insistent on responsible behavior, but a resolute adherence to standards has been out of fashion in education circles for more than thirty years."[3]

A true child-centered environment provides children with discipline, direction, and training to allow each child to grow up properly. Wise are those parents and schools preparing children for their future by providing intelligent guidance. What does character education do? It promotes core ethical values that teach children life-guiding principles for success, such as respect, trustworthiness, caring, fairness, responsibility, self-discipline, perseverance, citizenship, and courage. It's not religious indoctrination, even though practically all religions support such values. Character education provides intelligent guidance showing children the wisdom of doing things that will benefit them as well as society; however, there are many voices endorsing values that are detrimental to children.

Kids, Sex, and the Internet

One of the big debates among librarians is whether the Internet should have filters for children, and one of the big issues with parents is if they allow their children into libraries will they be permitted to view pornographic material. The American Library

Association Bill of Rights states, "A person's right to use a library should not be denied or abridged because of origin, age, background, or views." Then it further states, "Parents—and only parents—have the right and the responsibility to restrict the access of their children—and only their children—to library resources. Parents or legal guardians who do not want their children to have access to certain library services, materials or facilities, should so advise their children."[4]

Could you imagine elementary children in a school library having unlimited access to the Internet? This is why legislation is being enacted to mandate filtering devices to prevent children from viewing pornographic materials. The common-sense balance is so skewed that innocent and impressionable children are unprotected from viewing porn while review journals censor books teaching positive values under the guise they are didactic. What a double standard!

One of the saddest results of the "children should choose their own values" and "if it feels good, do it" philosophy is the ruinous effect of promiscuous sex. Millions are now infected with a wide assortment of venereal diseases because of living out the relativistic philosophy in their lives. Consider the plight of those infected with venereal diseases and the horrible disease of AIDS with its unrelenting attacks on the body. What do many schools do to combat these sexually transmitted diseases? The morally neutral teacher promotes "do-what-makes-you-feel-good," but use safe sex methods by always using a condom when having sex. They also promote homosexual and lesbian lifestyles as a method of avoiding pregnancy. If a girl becomes pregnant, she's taught the earlier she has an abortion the safer it is. The result? Children are increasingly putting into practice what they are learning. George F. Will, in the article, "Can't fix education until we fix families," reports:

> Family decomposition should dampen this week's self-congratulatory focus on the latest education legislation. In 1958 the percentage of children born to unmarried women was 5; in 1969, 10; in 1980, 18; in 1999, 33. The especially chilling number: in 1999 almost half (48.4 percent) of all children born to women ages 20-24—women of all races and ethnicities—were born out of wedlock.[5]

Think of this shocking statistic and the devastating impact this will have on the children and on the future of our nation that nearly half of "all children born to women ages 20-24—women of all races and ethnicities—were born out of wedlock."

Speaking about young mothers, Rosemary C. Salomone, Professor of Law at St. John's University School of Law, disclosed these facts:

> "Only seven out of 10 teenage mothers complete high school. Meanwhile, their

offspring are more likely to have low birth weight and other medical problems, and to be victims of abuse and neglect. Like their mothers, these children are twice as likely to drop out of school, twice as likely to have a child themselves in their teens, and one and a half times as likely to be out of work and school in their late teens and early 20s. And so the cycle continues."[6]

But mention abstinence—and many want to attack it as an archaic and unrealistic lifestyle. But abstinence until marriage produces healthy families. You would think schools would actively promote abstinence until marriage. There are some that do, but many cling to the relativistic philosophy that there are no moral absolutes. An article in *Time* magazine, "When Dating Is Dangerous," states, "One in five teenage girls reports being a victim of violence by her date." The article reports, "A recent study by the Harvard School of Public Health highlights how perilous adolescence can be, especially for girls." The comprehensive study of "high school girls shows that 1 in 5 reports being a victim of physical or sexual violence in a dating relationship. Girls reported being 'hit, slapped, shoved or forced into sexual activity' by dates."[7]

The *Houston Chronicle* writing about the report stated the research "stems from surveys of 4,163 public school students in Massachusetts, but the

authors say the results likely apply to teens nationwide....The study also suggests that a disturbing
number of adolescent boys 'have adopted attitudes
that men are entitled to control their girlfriends
through violence.'...More than 70 percent of the girls
who participated were white, about 10 percent were
Hispanic and about 6 percent each were black or
Asian." [8]

Many of these teenage boys are following the
values they were taught—"if it feels good, do it." The
victims? The girls who had been physically or sexually
abused—these girls the report states, are "about eight
to nine times more likely to have attempted suicide in
the previous year." [9] What can be done?

William Kilpatrick, Professor of Education at
Boston College, states in *Why Johnny Can't Tell Right
From Wrong:*

> The core problem facing our schools is
> a moral one. All other problems derive from
> it. Hence, all the various attempts at school
> reform are unlikely to succeed unless character
> education is put at the top of the agenda.
>
> If students don't learn self-discipline and
> respect for others, they will continue to exploit
> each other sexually no matter how many
> health clinics and condom distribution plans
> are created. [10]

Time in "An Rx for Teen Sex," and the subtitle,

"Doctors are joining the abstinence movement. Here's why they're now telling kids, 'Just say no.'" provides this report about Dr. Patricia Sulak, an obstetrician-gynecologist and professor at Texas A&M University's College of Medicine, who once advocated that kids should use condoms. Sulak now says, "But after reviewing the data, I've had to do a 180 on kids and sex." She has developed a sex-education curriculum where *Time* states "the lessons set forth the clinical consequences of teen sex in pictures and eye-popping statistics charting the numbers of young people infected with sexually transmitted diseases. The take-home message: abstain from intercourse or put yourself at grave medical risk."[11]

Houston Chronicle in "AIDS epidemic running rampant: Up to 46 million living with virus," states: "There was some positive news in the report, with several countries making progress in combating the spread of the disease. Uganda was considered one success story, marking its 12th consecutive year of reduced HIV infections."[12] CBC News from Canada tells what high school students in Uganda are hearing, "The kids are living through a national campaign against AIDS that's intensifying, not slowing, as proof grows that it's working. At their school near Kampala for instance, all students get tested regularly. Lectures are backed up with visits to hospital wards where they see AIDS patients dying."[13]

Namgura Jenfrancis, an Ugandan teacher reports, "They see a person suffering of AIDS, and sometimes they see a person dying. It's really scary. The kid has to feel it at heart and think, 'Okay, maybe the teachers are right, we should abstain.'"[14]

What's the message that's bringing success to Uganda in its fight against AIDS? It's the strong common-sense message of abstinence. Even the Centers for Disease Control and Prevention (CDC), once an advocate for condom use, has come out in favor of abstinence-only programs.[15]

The United States government offers this advice on their website for parents, "Tell them abstinence is the healthiest choice."[16] Houston Chronicle reports reactions to this advice. "That's dictating values, say organizations including the American Civil Liberties Union and gay rights groups, and they want the site taken down."[17] They also report that SIECUS, National Education Association, and over 100 other advocacy groups are wanting to have this website shut down.

But since when is America's position that we as a nation are without values? What do these organizations want? They want their values to be promoted. But abstinence until marriage would put a screeching halt to the rampant epidemic of sexually transmitted diseases.

There is hope that some after seeing the devastating effects of recreational sex are reconsidering their approach to sex education. One wonders how many more ruined lives it will take to cause schools to change.

Chapter 5
Character Education Movement

In spite of the anticultural movement, there is a strong cry across our nation from parents, teachers, and legislators that schools should teach character. Currently many states are mandating character education in public schools. The violence and shootings at schools have shocked the American public. Too many children trained in the relativistic philosophy of individual autonomy have turned into cruel monsters without a conscience. *Education Week* in "Youths' Lack of Values, Character Worries American Public," states:

> The American public is anxious about an apparent crisis in the moral well-being of children and teenagers, and parents and schools are largely to blame, a national survey has found.
>
> More than six in 10 adults, or 61 percent, said youngsters' failure to learn such values as honesty, respect, and responsibility is a very serious problem, according to the study. Only 37 percent believe today's children, once they're grown, will make the United States a better place.

"The traditional ideal of children as a source of renewal and hope has, for the majority of the American public, been seriously undermined," reports the study, "Kids These Days: What Americans Really Think About the Next Generation."...

Adults' overriding concern about children is not health problems, safety, or poverty—topics so often the focus of professional child advocates—but rather their character and values, the report says.[1]

Glen Elsasser of the *Chicago Tribune* also points out what is happening in schools concerning character education. He writes:

McGuffey's Readers offered literacy and lessons on the importance of obedience, honesty, kindness and thrift. But their popularity and use subsided, with the type of teaching they represented ebbing and flowing over the succeeding decades.

Now, at the end of the 1990's, a movement known as character education has gained obvious momentum and in the process is reviving what seem to be distinctly McGuffey-like values.

Unlike the days of McGuffey, however, the teaching of values and virtues has been expanded far beyond reading and writing classes to all academic subjects and extracurricular activities.

From the early days of the American republic, character and education were classroom verities—or as Diane Ravitch, a Brookings Institution fellow and New York University expert on education, said recently, character was always implicit in education.

The sources of the resurgence are varied: local schools, state education agencies and nonprofit organizations and foundations, with the federal government offering financial incentives to ensure that student values and ethics are part of the lesson plan.[2]

Traditional Values Taught

Prior to World War I, teaching of traditional values was common in public education. Then came the belief that since people were steadily improving, there was no need to teach traditional values. Bonnindell Clouse, professor of educational psychology at Indiana State University, pointed out, "The thirties, forties, and early fifties were a time of optimism based on a philosophy of social evolution that said that people are getting better and better. It seemed, therefore, that they did not need specific training to improve."[3]

I remember in the '30s when I attended public school that the teacher went around the room checking if we carried a handkerchief and if our fingernails were clean. As time went on, problems began: World War II, Korea, Vietnam, and dictators emerged and slaughtered millions. *Time* presents this report about philosopher Allan Bloom at the University of Chicago, from his provocative book, *The Closing of the American Mind*:

In Bloom's analysis, the universities went seriously off course in the 1960s, when they succumbed to pressures from student activists, feminists and black radicals for more "relevance" in the curriculum. This coalition hardened into a leftish tyranny whose demands, asserts Bloom, wounded American universities as sorely as right-wing assaults damaged German higher education during Hitler's rise. He defines the U.S. movement's essence, which he calls cultural relativism, as a half-digested export version of the nihilistic Nietzschean doctrine that underlay the trashing in Germany. Such relativism, says Bloom, broke down higher education's traditional role as defender of real enlightenment against society's ephemera, leaving the universities open to the "radical subjectivity of all belief about good and evil," as well as to a primacy of self that demanded equal time for anyone's own thing. This egalitarian "education of openness," as Bloom brands it, was a reform without content, accepting everything and denying the power of reason to pursue the common good....

He calls for a return to the reasoned insights to be gained from classical philosophy. He warns that for Americans, whose government was founded upon reason, the present "crisis in the university, the home of reason, is perhaps the profoundest crisis they face."[4]

In the seventies, there was a cry for values. The educational system responded. They presented values clarification as the way to plant values into the lives of children. Now parents could be relieved that schools were once again teaching values.

Values Clarification

Values clarification, however, was another subtle approach to incorporate relativism. *Values Clarification*, by Sidney B. Simon, Leland W. Howe, and Howard Kirschenbaum, acclaimed as the most widely known and used book in the new field of values education during that time, cites a strategy that "illustrates how difficult it is for any one teacher to say, 'I have the right values for other people's children.'" Here's a problem from their book:

> The Alligator River Story: Once upon a time there was a woman named Abigail who was in love with a man named Gregory. Gregory lived on the shore of a river. Abigail lived on the opposite shore of the river. The river which separated the two lovers was teeming with man-eating alligators. Abigail wanted to cross the river to be with Gregory. Unfortunately, the bridge had been washed out. So she went to ask Sinbad, a river boat captain, to take her across. He said he would be glad to if she would consent to go to bed with him preceding the voyage. She promptly refused and went to a friend named Ivan to explain her plight. Ivan did not want to be involved at all in the situation. Abigail felt her only alternative was to accept Sinbad's terms. Sinbad fulfilled his promise to Abigail and delivered her into the arms of Gregory.
>
> When she told Gregory about her amorous escapade in order to cross the river, Gregory cast her aside with disdain. Heartsick and dejected, Abigail turned to Slug with her tale of woe. Slug, feeling compassion for Abigail, sought out Gregory and beat him brutally.

Abigail was overjoyed at the sight of Gregory getting his due. As the sun sets on the horizon, we hear Abigail laughing at Gregory.[5]

After hearing this story, children are to "privately rank the five characters from the most offensive character to the least objectionable."[6] They are divided into groups of four to discuss the pros and cons of each character. Imagine immature boys and girls debating the pros and cons of sex to gain favor in a nonjudgmental atmosphere.

Other controversial moral issues are examined. One such activity is "survival games." Children are divided into groups. Suddenly World War III begins, with bombs dropping everywhere. People are running for shelters, and the class group is in charge of these shelters. A desperate call is received from a fallout shelter where ten people want to enter, but to survive the necessary three months there's enough space, air, food, and water for only six. The group has exactly one-half hour to decide which ones will enter before they themselves must seek protection. Here are the individuals:

1. Bookkeeper; 31 years old
2. His wife; six months pregnant
3. Black militant; second-year medical student
4. Famous historian-author; 42 years old
5. Hollywood starlette; singer; dancer
6. Bio-chemist

7. Rabbi; 54 years old
8. Olympic athlete; all sports
9. College co-ed
10. Policeman with gun (they cannot be
    separated)

The teacher distributes copies of this list to the class and then counts down: 15-, 10-, 5-, and then 1-minute warnings.[7] Instead of seeking ways to find out how to save all ten, children are asked to decide who will die. This is an ideal strategy to teach children early that it's permissible to kill certain individuals.

Autonomous Children

Everything children have been taught is taken apart and clarified: religion, sex, family, parents, feelings, attitudes, problems, etc. Nothing is personal or sacred. Children must be autonomous and decide freely, immature and unwise as they are and without parental input, their own set of values.

Values clarification often places children into dilemma situations in which they must make decisions between two wrong choices. It often deals with situations that in all likelihood will never happen, and some situations in which even philosophers would have difficulty in deciding what to do. Instead of teaching positive morality, it stresses situation ethics. Its effect destroys traditional values. Values clarification also indoctrinates children until they lose their sense of shame over evil and accept degenerate behavior as normal. The pros and cons of drugs, homosexuality, lesbianism, premarital sex, prostitution, lying, stealing, infanticide, euthanasia, and suicide are likely to be discussed while nonjudgmental teachers carefully avoid imposing their values.

Some will say, "You can't legislate morality," as an excuse to promote moral relativism. If one can't legislate morality, then one can't punish indecent behavior, cheating, stealing, and killing. Of course society must legislate morality. We can't let criminals run free or naked people run through our streets. Sensible laws are passed both for schools and society based on reason and common sense.

Others contend values should be taught at home and not in school. True, homes should play a major factor in teaching morals, but morals should be taught everywhere. Honesty, self-control, respect, responsibility, caring, courage, citizenship, etc, are values that should be encouraged everywhere; whereas cheating, lying, fighting, bullying, hating, etc., are negative values that should be condemned.

Governor Mike Huckabee of Arkansas said in his book, *Character Is the Issue*, "Our character defines the world we live in. Our government, welfare programs, schools, and everything else in our lives are shaped and directed according to our character...In fact every law in the country is a reflection of our moral values. We have laws against murder and stealing because we believe they are morally wrong."[8]

Others will criticize character education programs as ineffective. They will be if the schools are teaching character in the abstract. There must be a climate of character within the entire school. Teachers cannot expect students to be honest just because they had a lesson on honesty. If students cheat, they should be punished. If students disrupt classes, corrective action should be taken. If bullying takes place, the bullies need to be disciplined. Teachers and principals must be given the right to discipline unruly children. Sadly, educational leaders often tie the hands of teachers and principals in matters of discipline.

To contend schools should not teach values is impossible—all education in one form or another teaches values. Take American history: either one condemns slavery or one condones it. To remain neutral is in effect condoning slavery for those believing in slavery. If tests are given: either one condemns cheating or accepts it. Values are inherent in education. One cannot be morally neutral. The question should be asked—what values should be taught?

Character Education Programs Examined

The teachings of relativism have permeated our educational system. A teacher posed this problem to a group of eleven-year-old students, "What if you were eighteen years old and found yourself pregnant?" No guidance was given, except for one rule, "You may not say that any problem or solution is right or wrong." The teacher by saying, "You may not say that any problem or solution is right or wrong," is trying to be morally neutral and nonjudgmental; however, this is a definite moral position. It is moral relativism—there are no moral absolutes. Moral neutrality is an illusion—one cannot be morally neutral. Either you are for or against premarital sex. If you say, "I take no position on premarital sex," that's a moral decision saying it is proper for some to engage in premarital sex.

Moral relativism, under the guise of tolerance, is a serious attack on traditional values, and it threatens the very fabric of our society. Concerned individuals need to make sure that when schools speak of teaching character education they are not reviving values clarification where all values are personal, subjective, and relative, neither right or wrong. With such a value system, intolerance and tyranny can be chosen as virtues just as freedom, justice, and human dignity.

John Leo in *U.S. News & World Report* states, "73 percent of the students said that when their professors taught about ethical issues, the usual message was that uniform standards of right and wrong don't exist." Then he told of a college professor in upstate New York who "reported that 10 percent to

20 percent of his students could not bring themselves to criticize the Nazi extermination of Europe's Jews. Some students expressed personal distaste for what the Nazis did. But they were not willing to say that the Nazis were wrong, since no culture can be judged from the outside and no individual can challenge the moral worldview of another."[9]

In another article, Leo points out, "Overdosing on nonjudgmentalism is a growing problem in the schools. Two disturbing articles in the *Chronicle of Higher Education* say that some students are unwilling to oppose large moral horrors, including human sacrifice, ethnic cleansing, and slavery, because they think that no one has the right to criticize the moral views of another group or culture." Leo adds, "Christina Hoff Sommers, author and professor of philosophy at Clark University in Massachusetts, says that students who can't bring themselves to condemn the Holocaust will often say flatly that treating humans as superior to dogs and rodents is immoral. Moral shrugging may be on the rise, but old-fashioned and rigorous moral criticism is alive and well on certain selected issues: smoking, environmentalism, women's rights, animal rights."[10]

These nonjudgmentalists are being hypocritical by claiming no one has a right to judge others, while they judge others on selected issues. For example, Leo told of Kay Haugaard, a teacher of creative writing at Pasadena City College in California, who asked a student if she believed in human sacrifice. The woman replied, "I really don't know. If it was a religion of long standing...." Haugaard wrote, "I was stunned. This was the woman who wrote so passionately of saving the whales, of concern for the rain forests, of her rescue and tender care of a stray dog."[11]

One may be puzzled why some can be so passionate about saving whales, baby seals, and dogs, yet be advocates for homosexuality, lesbianism, euthanasia, infanticide, and abortion. Since humans are the enemy of the environment, any method to depopulate the earth is noteworthy.

One of the most shocking examples of loss of character in America is how members of Congress and even our former president supported the barbarous act of partial birth abortion. Imagine a perfectly innocent full-term baby ready to be born, and a doctor is lawfully permitted to puncture a hole into the child's skull and suck out its brain. Yet one minute later, if that same child happened to be out of the womb, that same act would constitute murder! Ancient civilizations had another way of getting rid of children; they threw them into a fire to appease their gods.

Tolerance is an excellent virtue when it concerns the treatment of people, but it is totally unacceptable when it states that all views are equally valid. Children should be taught to respect life and to oppose the moral horrors of human sacrifice, ethnic cleansing, and slavery. Unfortunately, there are those under the guise of teaching character education who do not support positive values. Concerned individuals need to make sure that the proper programs are implemented. The virtues that should be taught are the time-tested common sense values that have been passed down for thousands of years, such as respect, trustworthiness, caring, fairness, responsibility, self-discipline, perseverance, citizenship, and courage. "

Cultural War

We are in a cultural war — it's a conflict between the forces of relativism with its insistence on individual autonomy, and those believing in moral absolutes and individual responsibility. It's not just about immoral textbooks, sexual license, abortion, or violent movies and TV; it's much more. The conflict is over America's worldview in governing our nation.

We have yet to reap all the disastrous effects of this permissive immoral education implanted in the hearts and minds of our youth. Many of our youth today are filled with the detrimental hedonistic philosophy of moral relativism that brings havoc upon themselves and on our society. Much of the good left in America results from the inertia of our historic moral values, but this borrowing from the past cannot continue. There must be a renewal of historic virtues to keep America strong. Our earlier constitutional democracy inspired nations to emulate us.

We believe democracy is the answer for many nations of the world that are still dominated by dictators instead of the majority of the people. But one of the greatest hindrances of democracy is what's happening with our present brand of freedom that results in broken homes, violence, drug abuse, crime, juvenile delinquency, degenerate TV programs, perverted sex, and an epidemic of venereal diseases?

This is not the America that our Founding Fathers envisioned. Listen to what George Washington said in his first inaugural address: "The foundation of our national policy will be laid in the pure and immutable principles of private morality...the indissoluble union between virtue and happiness."[12] How many more nations would want to imitate our democracy if we lived by these principles?

William Kilpatrick in *Why Johnny Can't Tell Right From Wrong* cites this report of what's happening to many of the textbooks that children are reading:

On the elementary and high school level the stock of knowledge about right and wrong has dwindled even more drastically. In 1985 Professor Paul Vitz of New York University reported the results of a comprehensive study of ninety widely used elementary social studies texts, high school history texts, and elementary readers. What Vitz discovered was a "censorship by omission" in which basic themes and facts of the American and Western experience had been left out. Of the 670 stories from the readers used in grades three through six, only five dealt with any patriotic theme; moreover, "there are no stories that feature helping others or being concerned for others as intrinsically meaningful and valuable." "For the most part," writes Vitz, "these are stories for the 'me generation.'" More seriously, religion and marriage—institutions that have traditionally provided a context for learning morality—are neglected: None of the social studies books dealing with modern American social life mentioned the word "marriage," "wedding," "husband" or "wife."[13]

Can we let these shocking statistics sink in, "Of the 670 stories from the readers used in grades three through six, only five dealt with any patriotic theme," and "none of the social studies books dealing with modern American social life mentioned the word 'marriage,' 'wedding,' 'husband' or 'wife.'" There needs to be a moral outcry over what's happening in education today.

If the full implications of relativism were evident to the American people, they would be overwhelmingly opposed, and our historical value system would be restored. To counteract relativism, all Americans believing in the virtues that made our nation successful should boldly proclaim these morals and insist textbooks promote them also. But expect stiff opposition.

One of the favorite tactics of those believing in moral relativism is to label the opposition as bigoted, right wing, judgmental, intolerant, and one of their favorite ones: imposing religious values. By labeling the opposition in such terms, they don't have to explain or defend their position. But we mustn't let them silence us. The philosophy of relativism versus our historical value system is not only an issue for our schools, but also the major factors in how our country is governed. We must also reject judicial activism that seeks to rewrite our Constitution; instead, we need to diligently study the objectives of this historical document.

Today's fanatical obsession of separation of church and state is a perversion of the Constitution. A careful reading of the Constitution and the actions of Congress at that time clearly reveal what our Founding Fathers believed. The First Amendment of the Constitution, also called the Bill of Rights, states:

> Congress shall make no law respecting an establishment of religion, or prohibiting the free exercise thereof; or abridging the freedom of speech, or of the press, or the right of the people peaceably to assemble, and to petition the government for a redress of grievances.[14]

The Founding Fathers wanted to forbid the establishment of a national church by the federal government; they had no intention of limiting public religious expression. Notice that the Bill of Rights clearly states that Congress shall make no law "prohibiting the free exercise" of religion, "or abridging the freedom of speech." However, today it has been construed by many to mean that no teaching, views, insights, or values of the church can permeate or be accepted in public or governmental institutions. This position violates the very Bill of Rights it aims to protect by suppressing the rights of individuals to freely exercise their beliefs.

This emasculation of God from our country under the guise of "separation of Church and State," is not a constitutional concept. The character-building principles resulting from faith God has been the bedrock of our nation. We don't want a state church; but we should also not want a state totally devoid of belief in God. The First Amendment never intended to remove God from public life. To find out how our Founding Fathers felt about expressing God in public life, one must go to religious sources; secular forces have generally purged many of our historical documents from reaching the masses. (See www.wallbuilders. com)

Under President Clinton's administration, the United States Government published a paper on

Religious Expression in Public Schools: A Statement of Principles. These are several excerpts from that statement:

Student prayer and religious discussion: The Establishment Clause of the First Amendment does not prohibit purely private religious speech by students. Students therefore have the same right to engage in individual or group prayer and religious discussion during the school day as they do to engage in other comparable activity.

Teaching about religion: Public schools may not provide religious instruction, but they may teach about religion, including the Bible or other scripture: the history of religion, comparative religion, the Bible (or other scripture)-as-literature, and the role of religion in the history of the United States and other countries all are permissible public school subjects.

Student assignments: Students may express their beliefs about religion in the form of homework, art-work, and other written and oral assignments free of discrimination based on the religious content of their submissions.

Religious literature: Students have a right to distribute religious literature to their schoolmates on the same terms as they are permitted to distribute other literature that is unrelated to school curriculum or activities.

Teaching values: Though schools must be neutral with respect to religion, they may play an active role with respect to teaching civic values and virtue, and the moral code that holds us together as a community. The fact that some of these values are held also by religions does not make it unlawful to teach them in school.[15]

These guidelines state very clearly what teachers and students are allowed to do. Teachers cannot proselytize, but they have every right to allow religious expression in their classes. And in teaching character education, the guidelines specifically say, "The fact that some of these values are held also by religions does not make it unlawful to teach them in school."

Dr. Daniel Hade, Associate Professor of Education at Pennsylvania State University, and Dr. Jacqueline Edmondson, Assistant Professor of Education at the same school, stated in an article they co-authored, "Children's Book Publishing in Neoliberal Times":

Since the beginning of children's book publishing in the eighteenth century, children's books have provided children with entertainment and have contributed to the intellectual lives of children. But good children's literature can provide more than entertainment and an educated mind (Huck, 1982[16]). Children's literature can nurture children's spiritual lives as well. Through literature, children can experience the joys of being alive, find understanding and compassion for those who suffer, co-create with artists and authors using language and visual images, and transform joy into celebration and suffering into justice (Hade, 2002[17]). In other words, children can learn about being human.[18]

It's time for America to reject moral relativism and return to its traditional foundation of moral values. The future prosperity of our nation hinges on which philosophy gains ascendance. It is crucial for the dedicated few that understand that our national values should be based upon our moral heritage to go forth and stir the American people to action. There needs to be a moral cry from every hamlet, town, and city for the restoration of the historical values as provided by our Founding Fathers to bring our youth and nation out of moral chaos and disintegration.

Entrenched Bureaucracy

There are entrenched educational bureaucracies strongly opposed to our moral heritage. America needs a parental revolution to incorporate character education. Many teachers are unaware of the ramifications of their teaching methods; they have been trained in relativistic procedures and they continue to follow what they have been taught. They need to be provided with books and literature exposing the relativistic philosophy. Some teachers will change after learning the full implications of their teaching methods.

Concerned citizens cannot stand idly by and watch the systematic destruction of American youth become totally demoralized to the point of accepting perverted sex and degenerate behavior that current non-judgmental programs are propagating. Does America have an established value system? Absolutely! Americans need to rise up and promote virtues that are consistent with the beliefs our nation was founded upon and that made our nation great. These virtues have a proven track record.

Chapter 6
Actions to Promote
Educational Success

Having grown up in the '30s and early '40s in New York City, I never saw a prostitute or witnessed drug activity. My wife and sister as teenagers could ride the subways late at night and walk home in safety.

From the United States Information Agency comes this report about effects of the Great Depression. "In October 1929 the stock market crashed, wiping out 40 percent of the paper values of common stock. Even after the stock market collapse, however, politicians and industry leaders continued to issue optimistic predictions for the nation's economy. But the Depression deepened, confidence evaporated and many lost their life savings. By 1933 the value of stock on the New York Stock Exchange was less than a fifth of what it had been at its peak in 1929. Business houses closed their doors, factories shut down and banks failed. Farm income fell some 50 percent. By 1932 approximately one out of every four Americans was unemployed."[1]

Some like to blame poverty as a cause of our social problems. In the midst of the great poverty of the Great Depression, the public school teachers rated the top seven disciplinary problems in 1940 as: talking out of turn, chewing gum, making noise, running in the hall, cutting in line, dress code violations, and littering. Fifty years later when our country was much more prosperous, these were the top public school disciplinary problems: drug abuse, alcohol abuse, pregnancy, suicide, rape, robbery, and assault. What happened?

The permissive, "do-what-you-want" philosophy of moral relativism permeated our educational system. As a substitute teacher in 27 different public schools, I witnessed firsthand the fear of children sitting in these permissive, undisciplined jungles. From the 1940s to now, everything has changed. Now in the smallest towns doors must be locked, and it's unsafe for women to be out alone at night.

Those believing in moral relativism refuse to provide positive training for children. They have their buzzwords: they're for children's rights and tolerance. They teach children there are no moral absolutes and they should choose their own way. Then we wonder why so many choose destructive paths for themselves and for society.

What is the key to turning America around and bringing back civility and common sense standards of morality? One of the major keys is to insist that our children attend schools that implement programs promoting character which leads to educational success.

Four Keys for Successful Schools

The educational crisis facing America today is a philosophical crisis: should the inherent values of our educational system be based on moral relativism that there are no absolutes, or should our educational system be based on America's historical value system? There are four main crisis areas facing schools: educational, disciplinal, racial, and moral. The key to success in each of these areas has to do with which value system is chosen.

What would happen if educational leaders would declare from America's heritage this value from the Declaration of Independence?

> We hold these truths to be self-evident, that all men are created equal, that they are endowed by their Creator with certain unalienable Rights, that among these are Life, Liberty and the pursuit of Happiness.

As a consequence of our Constitution that all men are created equal, regardless of your color or background, *all* students must behave and respect every teacher and student in their desire of life, liberty and pursuit of happiness.

Could you envision the transformation of our schools if there would be a sign over every school entrance: "Once you enter these doors, we will *not* tolerate misbehavior!" Everything would be done to help misbehaving students, but those refusing to change—reform school.

I'm not endorsing carrying a bat and clobbering any kid who disobeys. That's how opponents would like to paint those believing in discipline. But proper discipline creates a loving atmosphere that refuses to tolerate misbehavior so that all students can receive the best education. Fair, firm, and loving discipline works wherever it's applied: classrooms, schools, families, or businesses. Effective discipline needs all three. Eliminate any one of these three principles of fair, firm, or loving, and discipline will be ineffective.

Some may ask, "Why are you so strong on discipline?" I'm strong on discipline because I've witnessed firsthand as a substitute teacher the frustration of teachers and the fear of children sitting in undisciplined classrooms. I've documented in my book, *Schools in Crisis: Training for Success or Failure?* the ruinous effect that undisciplined schools have on children's educational experience. In undisciplined schools might makes right, and bullies becomes the leaders.

It's the same in the home. With 14 grandchildren I get many opportunities to watch them. Children demand justice. If Zachary acts as a bully and grabs a toy from his brother Nathan, Nathan will yell, "That's my toy!"

Nathan is right to object. If I act as a loving grandpa, I'll demand justice that each child must respect the rights of others. I'll tell Zachary, "No, you can't take a toy from Nathan." And if Zachary does this again, I will punish him and put him in timeout. Zachary will learn that in grandpa's house bullying will not be tolerated. If I don't intervene and demand justice, then the rule of the jungle will prevail—the weak will be exploited by the strong. This will cause constant friction.

It's the same with schools. All the lofty goals of leaving no child behind can never be achieved unless schools are disciplined. Effective education is only possible in a disciplined atmosphere. Others may contend, "You're much too hard. What about children's rights?" That's exactly the problem. What about the rights of the innocent children being deprived of a proper education? What about the right of not being abused by bullies? Put yourself into the shoes of those who are bullied.

Listen to how it affected Erika Harold, who was chosen Miss America. Harold has been so affected by bullying that she goes on speaking tours telling about her experience of being bullied in ninth grade. "It started out with people calling me names, and then it got worse," Harold said. "They threw things at me, they vandalized my house, and they sang nasty songs about me in school hallways and classrooms. It got so bad that I felt like I was in danger physically."[2]

What about Miss America's rights when she was bullied in ninth grade? Fight Crime: Invest in Kids, a national advocacy group that consists of over 2,000 law enforcement officers and victims of violence, reports that each year for children in grades six through ten nearly one in six, or 3.2 million, were victims of bullying and 3.7 million were bullies. Of those labeled as bullies in grades six through nine, nearly 60 percent of the boys were convicted of one crime by the time they reached 24. Those bullied, the report stated, citing U.S. and European studies, are five times more prone to be depressed and more likely to be suicidal.[3] A study by Vanderbilt University estimates that each high-risk juvenile that is saved from a life of crime would save the country from $1.7 to $2.3 million.[4] What would happen if *all* schools would implement a fair, firm, and loving discipline policy?

Governor of Arkansas, Mike Huckabee, points out in his book, *Character Is the Issue*, the consequences of lack of values:

> If Arkansas is going to be the great state that it can be and must be, we must put Arkansas first in underscoring responsibility. I believe we focus so many times only on revenues. Today I'll offer a new paradigm of government, suggesting that maybe we've misplaced priorities, believing that what we do with

the cash is more important than what we do with character. Let me be blunt and say that all the problems we face in our society are not monetary. Quite a few are moral.

We're going to be criticized for even suggesting that is really the core of the problem. But my friends, I'd rather be criticized for being honest with the real problems than for ignoring them. And I submit to you today that falling test scores, illegitimacy, drug and alcohol dependence, crime, and domestic violence are really symptoms of a crisis of integrity far more than just a crisis of cash....

Our rate of illegitimacy in Arkansas is too high. The fact is that 88 percent of the women who have a child out of wedlock and never finish high school will end up in poverty. And we will end up paying for them in welfare benefits. Interestingly enough, only 8 percent of women who finish high school, get married, and have a baby after the age of 20 will ever be in poverty. It seems to me that if we want a 92 percent success rate in dealing with some of the problems, let's make sure that our students finish school, let's make sure that they understand the responsibilities of a marriage, and let's make sure that they understand the responsibilities of bringing a child into this world. And that involves dealing with character.

A young male is twice as likely to be involved in criminal activity if he has no father in the home and three times as likely to be involved in criminal activity if he comes from a neighborhood where the majority are single-parent families. It's costly, my friends, when we ignore this issue....

It can cost us as much as $40,000 a year to take care of one juvenile who has fallen into delinquency....The cost of the state courts in the past decade has risen from $6.2 million to $17.2 million. The more crime we have, the more prison beds we have to create at a cost of about $22,000 per bed—$77 million more in prison expenditures in the past decade. All of that is money that ought to be, could be, should be going for better education, for better highways, for a better atmosphere that we could live in...The sad thing is that as long as we continue to spend money addressing the symptoms rather than addressing the root cause, we may always be thinking that it's just a matter of money when the truth is that it is also the matter of us taking the leadership and believing that integrity is important and it's got to start somewhere.[5]

Are we getting the picture of the great social cost for lack of character? Money that could be spent for bettering the life of citizens must be spent on those who have not been trained in character.

In the early 1980s, two social scientists advocated what became known as the broken-window theory. They claimed that if a broken window was not fixed in a neighborhood, other windows in the neighborhood would likewise be smashed. Why? It sent a message that no one cared. This produced further vandalism and criminal-minded individuals would be attracted while law-abiding citizens would leave. The key was to immediately fix the broken window. Charles Colson in his book, *How Now Shall We Live?* cites what happened when New York City implemented the broken-window theory:[6]

In the early 1990s, New York Police Chief William Bratton took the broken-window theory to heart and persuaded New York's newly elected mayor and tough ex-prosecutor Rudolph Guiliani to give the theory a try. The order went out to police in Precincts 69 and 75 and to Brooklyn, where Officer Sal was stationed, to 'fix broken windows'—that is, to arrest petty offenders and clean up the neighborhoods. The police adopted a policy of zero tolerance for any violation of public order, and in the process they soon discovered that there is indeed a 'seamless web' between controlling petty crime and restraining major crime. Whereas before they had ignored turnstile jumping at subways, officers now nabbed the offenders, who, as often as not, turned out to be muggers. Whereas before they had turned a blind eye to minor traffic violations, they now stopped all traffic violators, which often led to the discovery of drugs and guns in the cars. They chased away loiterers and panhandlers, many of whom were drug dealers looking for a sale. In three years in Precinct 75, once one of the most dangerous places in America, the number of homicides dropped from 129 to 47.[7]

How many school problems would evaporate if administrators would insist that every student respects the rights of others and if "zero tolerance" would be implemented for misbehavior? That would send a strong message about the character virtue of respecting others.

Schools should also provide programs that every child, regardless of race or color, has the opportunity to achieve his or her fullest constitutional right to life, liberty, and the pursuit of happiness. Standards for each grade should be implemented, materials should be provided that teach and encourage children to reach their full potential, and teachers should be evaluated on their teaching.

Those opposed to such programs would like to portray this as being judgmental and as forcing one's beliefs on children. They present themselves as champions of being nonjudgmental and of supporting individual liberty. It's the exact opposite—this method creates an environment where *all* children can be taught the values of how they can become successful and enjoy their full liberty. Those opposed to training children in proper behavior, in their perverted view of liberty, allow children in undisciplined schools and permissive learning environments to fall further and further behind. The result? Today, America ranks close to the bottom in the industrialized world in educational achievement.

Here are four keys to successful schools:

1. Educational: Insist that every child receive a proper education by providing appropriate teaching materials for every grade, eliminating automatic promotion, administering standards for every grade, and evaluating teachers.

2. Disciplinal: Insist that every school provide a disciplined learning environment so children are protected and can receive a proper education.

3. Racial: Create a learning atmosphere that treats all races the same, and provide resources so all children can reach their full potential.

4. Moral: Reject moral relativism by

providing textbooks that teach the values that built our nation, and promote virtues that help children develop successful habits.

I could go into much detail about the educational, disciplinal, racial, and moral solutions. I addressed these issues in detail in the 335-page book I wrote: *Schools in Crisis: Training for Success or Failure?* The book is available free on our website.[8] The book provides many principles for successful schools that are still applicable.

Our Founding Fathers built this nation because they believed in values. They did not believe in moral relativism. My hope is that Americans will wake up and return to our constitutional heritage. Imagine what would happen if educational leaders would implement these four steps for successful schools across America. I know there are strong forces opposed to these common-sense methods. It's much easier to take a permissive hands-off policy and let schools and children find their own way. Concerned individuals must insist that something be done that American schools can once again become models of achievement and promote the values that made our nation successful.

Schools Making a Difference

But there are schools, principals, and teachers who

believe in values, and they are making a difference. Trevor Armbrister, in "Principals of Success," reports that *Reader's Digest* visited four schools "where inspired leadership, innovative programs and old-fashioned values have resulted in small miracles of achievement." Here's one report:

The 1650 students at Bennett-Kew and Kelso elementary school in Inglewood, Calif., are predominantly Hispanic and African American. Most of them are poor, and about half speak English as a second language. Still, they performed almost as well as affluent counterparts....

It wasn't always this way. When Ichinaga became principal of Bennett in 1974, the school, near Los Angeles International Airport, was in chaos. There were few textbooks and no defined curriculum. Students did their own thing—and scored at the third percentile on state reading tests. According to Ichinaga, teachers shrugged, as if to say, "What did you expect?"....

Ichinaga, who grew up in Hawaii, found a kindred spirit in Marjorie Thompson, a transplanted Kentuckian and principal of nearby Kelso Elementary. Together they rebelled against low expectations and fashionable educational trends.

Resisting efforts to "dumb down" what they taught, both principals instituted a rigorous core curriculum centered on reading, writing and math. Convinced that reading was the critical skill for their kids, Ichinaga and Thompson began using a structured, phonics-based language-arts program called Open Court. The results have been impressive....

Ichinaga and Thompson also said no to social promotions, meaning they wouldn't allow failing kids to move automatically to the next grade....

It took years, but many Californians have come to agree that Ichinaga and Thompson were right about a lot of things. That includes former state school superintendent Bill Honig, who was calling the shots when "whole language" was adopted. "Many kids never learned to read," he says. "To the extent whole language stood in many teachers' minds for not teaching [basic] skills, it caused a lot of harm."[9]

Notice these two principals "rebelled against low expectations" to "dumb down" the curriculum and instituted the time-tested method of phonics to teach reading. They also rejected the easy route of social promotions and applied "old-fashioned values" with a belief that all kids can learn.

In *A Gift of Character: The Chattanooga Story*, Dr. Philip Fitch Vincent, Nancy Reed, and Dr. Jesse Register relate what happened when the Hamilton County School District, with 44 elementary schools, 15 middle schools, 10 high schools, and 9 special schools integrated character education into the school curriculum.

Before a character education program was implemented, they wanted to reject the failures of values clarification that morals are relative and the weaknesses of the self-esteem movement that promotes false hopes. The authors stated: "We must instill in students a knowledge and love of the good. We must develop rules and procedures to insure a good climate for learning. In short, a school must have standards, and values clarification provides none." Then the authors pointed out: "Next in training, we addressed the false promise of the self-esteem movement as a means to help students develop civic and virtuous traits. We recognized that *feeling* good is not the same as *being* good."[10] The school district established these principles:

1. Establishment of Rules and Procedures for behavior.

2. Cooperative Learning where students work together.

3. Teaching for Thinking so students use reasoning skills to develop character.

4. Reading for Character where students read

literature "that is worth reading and that provides strong examples of good character."

5. Service Learning where students are encouraged to help others both within and outside the school.[11]

They enlisted the representatives of the community and businesses, and sent 800 letters to ministers and religious youth leaders of various faiths inviting them to a meeting to discuss the district's character initiative. They provided training for superintendents and their representatives, principals, guidance counselors, and teachers. Schools were encouraged to develop their own character education programs. The reports received from elementary, middle, and high schools showed some schools with a decrease in office referrals and suspensions up to 300%; less fighting, stealing, and other violent offenses; more lost items returned; and students eager to help teachers and others.

A school stated in its report: "Character education is not presented as a separate subject for our children to learn. The message of this curriculum is integrated throughout the day by all of the employees of the school, and our children are reminded of the character traits everywhere they go. Teachers include discussions and activities about character in every academic subject from reading to math to social studies."[12]

This is an important point to those supporting character education. Character education should not be just an isolated lesson on a certain character trait;

character education should be a program that infiltrates the entire curriculum.

Another school noted: "We integrated character education into every aspect of our school. This integration included curriculum, music, guidance, library, cafeteria, physical education, programs, discipline plans, newsletters, and PTO meetings. Guest speakers have come, and entire assemblies have been devoted to character."[13]

Character education works when proper values are stressed. Tim Stafford, in "Helping Johnny Be Good," reports that San Marcos Junior High won the California Distinguished School Award. Ten years ago the school had a crisis: more than one out of five girls were pregnant. To counter this, San Marcos Junior High began a comprehensive character education program, including one of the first abstinence-based sex education programs and the "How to Be Successful" program. These programs were successful. Pregnancies decreased dramatically even though the student population increased. Skeptical teachers were won over after they witnessed the fruits of success from these programs.[14]

U.S. News & World Report in "Morality goes to schools" states about character education: "There's no shortage of compelling testimonials. 'It's like night and day' at the 30 Dallas public schools that instituted Character Counts! five years ago, says Linda Jones, who oversees the project at the Dallas Independent

School District. 'The whole emotional atmosphere of the building changes. It becomes a kinder, gentler place.' Other schools have seen fights and suspensions plummet."[15]

In "Character Education Is Back in Our Public Schools," Michael Josephson reported that "South Dakota State University surveyed 7,000 to 8,000 students and concluded" that Character Counts "helped cut crime, drug use, drinking, and other socially harmful activities sharply."[16]

Actions by Educators

There are administrators, principals, guidance counselors, librarians, and teachers who believe in our heritage and value system and are alarmed at the deterioration of our schools. Individually they often feel helpless to change the entrenched relativistic bureaucracy. John Leo, in *U.S. News & World Report*, states this chilling fact: "A study by the Public Agenda research group found that only 7 percent of education professors think teachers should be conveyers of knowledge; 92 percent believe teachers should just 'enable students to learn on their own.' Hymowitz thinks anticulturalism explains why bad schools fight so tenaciously to hold on to failed programs: They are more deeply interested in ideology than in results."[17]

Yes, in spite of documented failure, there are powerful forces who cling to their ideology of advocating the permissive route of leaving students to learn on their own and opposing teaching children successful values. Nevertheless, administrators, principals, guidance counselors, librarians, teachers, and parents need to speak out boldly and implement principles of educational success and moral virtues, even if it's just locally in their class or school. There are numerous resources for character education. At our website is information about character education organizations under "Free Resources." In addition, educators and concerned individuals need to become active and write to their organizations and other institutions when they promote values they deem inappropriate. We *must* let our voices be heard.

Actions by Parents

One of the most important things parents can do is to discipline their children and train them in positive values, and not simply rely on the schools to do the job for them. Parents need to have moral standards and teach them to their children. Above all, parents need to "walk the talk." Children will imitate us regardless of how much we teach them otherwise. Today, parents must be extremely careful they don't succumb to the deadly moral standards that are so popularized on TV, in music, children's magazines, and our present culture of letting children be free to develop their own values. Children need guidance; wise are those parents who supervise their children, provide positive materials, and take time to teach them successful virtues.

Parents need to be concerned that the schools their children attend support character education. If they don't, become an active voice for character education: encourage the librarian to purchase character-building books, become active in PTA, speak to the principal, and write to the superintendent. Let your voice be heard.

Men and Women of Action

What transpires in schools has repercussions far beyond classrooms; it affects every aspect of our national life. Every culture to survive must transmit its beliefs and values to the next generation. America, particularly the schools, has seriously departed from our historical beliefs and values and embraced an alien philosophy causing a crisis in our society.

Governor Mike Huckabee in his book, *Character Is the Issue*, stated:

There's a continuing debate about why American society has renounced its traditional standards of integrity. Many people agree that as a nation we once recognized a common standard and that somehow we've drifted away from it. The "right thing" today is subjective, which has caused problems with everything from discipline in the schools to pornography on the Internet.

How did we move in one generation from a society with a shared, confident sense of right to a society of relativism and moral decay?

No Single Answer

The first step to answering that question is to admit there isn't just one answer....If any force is going to overcome a free, prosperous country like America, it won't happen all at once. America has a solid foundation of liberty, personal dignity, and opportunity. Anybody can rise above his social circumstances. There's no caste system. You don't have to be a member of nobility to get ahead.

The only way to destroy something with that kind of foundation is to chip away at it, one value at a time. Take away its heart and essence. Bring doubt to what used to be confidence, denial to what used to be faith, death to what was life. I think that is what has happened.

Contrast that of the Great Depression with the generation of today. During the Depression, people were poor, hungry, and out of work. Yet they didn't engage in the kind of gang violence we have in our schools today. Students weren't killing each other for a pair of shoes. Crime could easily have been justified by saying, "I'm hungry, and I don't have as much as you; therefore, I have a right to take what I can get." Dishonesty was still considered wrong, and thieves were despised. [18]

Then Governor Huckabee pointed out, "Public officials and the policies they set show how far we have drifted, one tiny step at a time."[19] That's the key to bringing America back to its foundational strength, "one step at a time," even if they are tiny steps.

Governor Huckabee put his words into action. He instituted character education in public schools to teach children "age-old manners such as manners and respect for others."[20]

What we have in America today is a clash of worldviews. We constantly witness the polarization in the arts, politics, business, media, and education. Do we believe in the moral absolutes that America was founded upon or moral relativism? For a bright future for America, both economically and socially, we need to return to our foundational roots and restore the principles that made our nation successful. Since our nation's future will be largely determined by how the upcoming generation is taught, an important place to start is by training our children with positive values.

I urge everyone to become involved in the education of children. It has been said, "What you put into the school will appear in the life of the people of the next generation." We *must* provide children with an education in keeping with the standards that have made our nation successful. We should never forget the future pain and suffering these children will encounter because of the destructive effects of their inadequate moral learning experience.

I want to also stress the social and economic impact when character is not a national priority. Taxpayers must pay billions of dollars because of lack of character training resulting in drug abuse, assault, robbery, rape, venereal diseases, illegitimate children, alcohol abuse, and other socially harmful activities. Money that could be much better spent on improving education, building safer highways, and providing better health care for the masses. Who will arise to call America back to her foundational strengths? The issues are clearly marked; the lines are drawn.

There is hope. On September 11, 2001, terrorists, in hopes of discouraging Americans, targeted our nation and with four planes flew into the World Trade Center, The Pentagon, and crashed into an open field and within a few hours murdered over 3,000 innocent people. That tragic event brought a new awakening to Americans. There is good and evil, and we as Americans have a value system that we're willing to defend. Nine days after the terrorists attack, President George W. Bush, addressing a Joint Session of the U.S. Congress put out this challenge:

> Americans are asking: What is expected of us? I ask you to live your lives, and hug your children....I ask you to uphold the values of America, and remember why so many have come here. We are in a fight for our principles, and our first responsibility is to live by them.

Let's hug our children and join the fight to uphold the values of America. We must not become discouraged over the entrenched bureaucracy or by their favorite attack of labeling opponents as bigoted and intolerant. We must not tolerate the idea that teaching character is unacceptable. Every small step in the right direction is a victory.

There is hope as parents, teachers, librarians, principals, superintendents, and those in authority insist our moral heritage and its values are taught in our schools. Everyone needs to be on the offensive and reject the relativistic philosophy; the future of our nation hinges on the values of its children.

Let each of us take the mantle of responsibility to transform American education into a system producing educated, moral citizens. Our action or inaction will determine what happens to our great nation.

Notes

Chapter 1
Why I Am Writing This Book

[1] Tony Snow, "Struggle is between government and morality," *Houston Chronicle*, January 3, 1996.
[2] U.S. Department of Justice, www.ojp.usdoj.gov/bjs/eande.htm
[3] Ibid.
[4] Department of Health and Human Services, www.cdc.gov/std/stats/trends2003.htm
[5] U.S. Government Office of National Drug Control Policy, www.ncjrs.org/ondcppubs/publications/drugabuse/le.htm
[6] Carl Sommer, *Schools in Crisis: Training for Success or Failure?*, Houston, TX, Advance Publishing, 1984, available free online at www.advancepublishing.com see "Free Resources."

Chapter 2
Strong Oppositions

[1] "A Reviewer's Eye View" *Children's Writer*, June 1997.
[2] *The Horn Book Guide*, July-December, 2000.
[3] *School Library Journal*, August 2003.
[4] Book Publishers, *Writer's Digest*, September 1995.
[5] "Animals with Something to Say," *Children's Writer*, June 1996.
[6] "U.S. Seen Losing Edge on Education Measures," *Education Week*, April 4, 2001.
[7] Dr. Joseph H. Boyett and Jimmie T. Boyett, *The Guru Guide*, New York: John Wiley & Sons, 1998, pp. 321-322.
[8] "How China will change your business," Inc. Magazine, March 2005.
[9] David Gergen, "Will America Slip from No. 1?" *U.S News & World Report*, April 4, 2005.

[10] Ibid.

[11] Ibid.

[12] John Leo, "Don't listen to Miranda," *U.S. News & World Report*, June 16,1997.

[13] Ibid.

Chapter 3
The Philosophical Battle

[1] *Humanist Manifesto I & II*, American Humanist Association, Buffalo, New York: Prometheus Books, 1973.

[2] William Kilpatrick, *Why Johnny Can't Tell Right From Wrong*, New York: Touchstone (Published by Simon & Schuster), 1992, p. 155.

[3] Ibid. p. 157.

[4] "Corrections population tops record," *Houston Chronicle*, August 27, 2001.

[5] "Penal chief urges early rooting out of criminals," *Houston Chronicle*, December 28, 1997.

[6] *U.S. News & World Report*, "The American Uncivil Wars—How crude, rude and obnoxious behavior has replaced good manners and why that hurts our politics and culture," April 22, 1996.

[7] David G. Myers, "Wanting More In an Age of Plenty," *Christianity Today*, April 24, 2000.

[8] Mortimer B. Zuckerman, "Where Have Our Values Gone?" *U.S. News & World Report*, August 8, 1994.

[9] William Kilpatrick, *Why Johnny Can't Tell Right From Wrong*, New York: Touchstone (Published by Simon & Schuster), 1992, p. 136.

[10] Deborah Gitlitz, *Youth Services Librarian*, Lacey Timberland Library, Lacey, WA.

[11] Jenny Holloman, *Media Specialist*, Fairington Elementary

School, Lithonia, GA.

[12] *School Library Journal*, from Amazon.com website. Judith Vigna, "My Two Uncles."

[13] *Publisher Weekly*, from Amazon.com website. Michael Willhoite, "Daddy's Roommate."

[14] *School Library Journal*, from Amazon.com website. Michael Willhoite, "Daddy's Roommate."

[15] "Silence v. truth," *Citizen*, April 2005.

Chapter 4
Anticulturalism

[1] John Leo, "Parent-free zone," *U.S. News & World Report*, November 1, 1999.

[2] William J. Bennett, "Teaching the Virtues," *Imprimis*, February 2003.

[3] "How Moral Education Is Finding Its Way Back into America's Schools," William Damon, editor, *Bringing In a New Era In Character Education*, Stanford, California, Hoover Institution Press, 2002, p. 35.

[4] "The Library Bill of Rights," Adopted June 18, 1948 and reaffirmed January 23, 1996 by the American Library Association Council. Copies received at the ALA Convention, San Francisco, May 2001.

[5] "Can't fix education until we fix families," *Houston Chronicle*, January 6, 2002.

[6] Rosemary C. Salomone, "Single-Sex Programs for At-Risk Students," *Education Week*, September 10, 2003.

[7] "When Dating Is Dangerous," *Time*, August 27, 2001.

[8] "Study indicates date violence affects 1 in 5 high school girls," *Houston Chronicle*, August 1, 2001.

[9] Ibid.

[10] William Kilpatrick, *Why Johnny Can't Tell Right From Wrong*, New York: Touchstone (Published by Simon & Schuster), 1992, p. 225.

[11] "An Rx for Teen Sex," *Time*, October 7, 2002.

[12] "AIDS epidemic running rampant: Up to 46 million living with virus," *Houston Chronicle*, November, 26, 2003.

[13] "AIDS in Uganda: While AIDS is out of control in most of Africa, infection rates are dropping in Uganda," *CBC News*, December, 16, 2002.

[14] Ibid.

[15] "An Rx for Teen Sex," *Time*, October 7, 2002.

[16] http://www.4parents.gov/downloads/parentguide.txt. See www.4parents.gov for additional information.

[17] "Government Web site touts sexual abstinence," *Houston Chronicle*, April 1, 2005.

Chapter 5
Character Education Movement

[1] "Youths' Lack of Values, Character Worries American Public," *Education Week*, July 9, 1997.

[2] "Old-fashioned character building sees a revival at end of the century," *Houston Chronicle*, September 5, 1999.

[3] Bonnidell Clouse, "Reading, Writing, And... Right From Wrong?" *Christianity Today*, Dec. 30, 1977.

[4] "Nietzsche by Another Name," *Time*, April 13,1987.

[5] Sidney B. Simon, Leland W. Howe, and Howard Kirschenbaum, *Values Clarification*, New York: Hart Publishing Co., 1972, pp. 290-292.

[6] Ibid. p. 290.

[7] Ibid. p. 281-283.

[8] Mike Huckabee, *Character Is the Issue*, Nashville: Broadman & Holman Publishers, 1997, p. 1.

[9] John Leo, "Professors who see no evil," *U.S. News & World Report*, July 22, 2002.

[10] "A no-fault Holocaust," *U.S. News & World Report*, July 21, 1997.

[11] Ibid.

[12] Tony Snow, "Struggle is between government and morality," *Houston Chronicle*, January 3, 1996.

[13] William Kilpatrick, *Why Johnny Can't Tell Right From Wrong*, New York: Touchstone (Published by Simon & Schuster), 1992, p. 120.

[14] The Bill of Rights can be seen at: www.archives.gov/national_archives_experience/bill_of_rights_transcript

[15] *Religious Expression In Public Schools*, U.S. Department of Education, June 1998, pp. 4-5. The document can be viewed at: www.ed.gov

[16] "Children's Book Publishing in Neoliberal Times," *Language Arts*, National Council of Teachers of English, November 2003. (Huck, C.S., *Theory into Practice*, pp. 21, 315-321.)

[17] Ibid. (Hade, D.D., *The New Advocate*, pp. 15, 293-302.)

[18] "Children's Book Publishing in Neoliberal Times," *Language Arts*, National Council of Teachers of English, November 2003.

Chapter 6
Actions to Promote Character Education

[1] United States Information Agency, www.usemb.se/usis/history/chapter9.html

[2] Bullying not just kid's burden, *Houston Chronicle*, September 6, 2003.

[3] Ibid.

[4] Ibid.

[5] Mike Huckabee, Character Is the Issue, Nashville: Broadman &

Holman Publishers, 1997, pp. 175-177.

[6] Charles Colson, *How Now Shall We Live?* Wheaton, Illinois, Tyndale House Publishers, 1999, pp. 363-364.

[7] Ibid. p. 364.

[8] Carl Sommer, *Schools in Crisis: Training for Success or Failure?* Houston, TX Advance Publishing, 1984, available free online at www.advancepublishing.com, see "Free Resources."

[9] Trevor Armbrister, "Principals of Success," *Readers Digest,* February 2001.

[10] Dr. Philip Fitch Vincent, Nancy Reed, and Dr. Jesse Register, *A Gift of Character: The Chattanooga Story,* Chapel Hill, North Carolina, Character Development Publishing, 2001, p. 9.

[11] Ibid. pp. 10-12.

[12] Ibid. p. 87.

[13] Ibid. p. 105.

[14] Ibid.

[15] "Morality goes to school," *U.S. News & World Report,* June 4, 2001.

[16] Michael Josephson, "Character Education Is Back in Our Public Schools," *The State Education Standard,* Autumn, 2002.

[17] John Leo, "Parent-free zone," *U.S. News & World Report,* November 1,1999.

[18] Mike Huckabee, Character Is the Issue, Nashville: Broadman & Holman Publishers, 1997, pp. 175-177.

[19] Ibid. p. 95.

[20] Governor Huckabee/s News Column, August 7, 1999, www.arkansas.gov/governor/media/columns/text/c080799.html

Index